OLD PATH

Published by Dreaming Deer Press
Marietta, GA, USA 30067

ISBN-13: 9780692636213

ISBN-10: 0692636218

Cover art by Emily Lupita, watercolor & ink, 2004.

Printed in the United States of America

For poetry books, CDs & DVDs
by Joseph S. Plum, please visit:

www.JoePlum.com

Old Path

Joseph S. Plum

Dreaming Deer Press

Preface

The poems written in this book were transcribed from the original oral poetry that was crafted in the bardic tradition of dreaming and living a lifetime in connection with nature. The hope is that by writing down the poems and collecting them into books, they may travel widely and be shared with the world. If you have a chance, please say these poems aloud. In this way, the beauty and power of traditional bardic poetry will live on through your voice.

Artist's Statement

who will take a walk with me
down to the edge of an inward sea?
stand there – look to see
straight through a whirlpool of uncertainty
right into the heart of eternity!

-Joseph Samuel Plum
from *waterfall*

Contents

spirit land..1

old path..5

comes a moment..7

heaven's company..15

separate entity..21

banquet of winter..27

margaret rose..31

portage of the soul..33

taken to raise...39

twice born..43

this...45

passage back...49

quadrants...53

for Water

spirit land

     spirits

come see what you've done to me

spirits

come see what you've done

spirits

come see

spirits

come

     spirits come see

what you've done to me

right from the start

while handing out ecstasy

you were taking my heart

by touching my soul

you crushed me to the bone

until now

i no longer have feelings

that are even my own

in visions which burn

and dance in my head

spirits bring back to life legends

from the land of the dead

greetings they say

to you and your kind

we welcome your body

to the battle

between timing and time.

   vital is the wave

which carries the wise

fierce are the rays

from the sun in my eyes

faceless is the smile

of those who survive

spirits that come

and enter their lives

     earthlings of another order

everyday reach out to me

from beyond the borders

of their shadowland's

boundary waters

caught in the principle

of the flow

one way conversations

let me know

that if now is when

to be letting go

then there in

is where waits

the rest of my soul

begging for spirits

to come here

and make me whole

    spirits

please come to me

and grace me faithfully

with moments based instinctively

on the glory of innate majesty

for every movement

here on earth

is but a shadow dance

extending through

the synchronicity of circumstance

our one real ghost of a chance

to entice with sweat

the allies we lack

so as to outlive this struggle

with our integrity intact

and thereby win

the secret of enlightened passage back

from you spirits

who have kept us

so long in the black

without even a horizon

to show us

where it is we're at

    spirits

please come to me

and tell me truthfully

what is so wrong

with knowing so little

of how to live

away from the middle

of a world broken

open at the seams

by the birthing contractions

of sleeping time beings.

old path

too many roads

when the old path is waiting

no need for mentality

while the heart is debating

the way of remembrance

versus everyday living

as the beauty of this moment

comes wrapped in lifetimes

of eternity forgiving

the changelings of night

for the darkness they're carrying

and the children of light

for the burden of shadows they're sharing

with those who would rather

be reaching beyond

the crosses they're bearing

to uphold the sky

while they drink in the earth

to go out in feeling

until they come back in birth

to sing with brightness

of the ancient ways

to bring in with lightness

the dawn

of all our future days

    yes, there are too many roads

when the old path is calling

too many roads

once the pale sky starts falling.

comes a moment

listen.
our language encircles us
with prisms of knowledge
that break clear light
into pyramids of color
and threads of darkness.
by the hand of our faith,
together with truth,
these words are woven into lies
on the loom of desire
until we are wrapped
in a silk of unbroken reflections
against which our fresh
and untried wings
push!

in a wordless way
rain washes dust
from ten thousand days,
while in evening's deep
and dreamless cool,

crickets dance and drink

from morning's crystal dew.

black red wing birds

and flutter bys,

thunder poems

sung in dragonfly,

dusty fingers stalk the moon

to trace a pillowed sky

as a setting sun of ashen hue

tells this world good bye.

up from across a sea of satin breeze

ageless anthems roll,

misleading those who would be led,

overturning my empty bowl.

    yes, i have no faith

in firm belief,

said the night mist to the wind.

in passing over

the depths of winter's sky,

the stars of spring shine in.

yes, i have no faith

in winter's spring

or in summer's sudden fall.

just on the grounds
of what is see,
i have no faith at all.
and yet against the skies
of what i feel
my eternal spirit sails,
bringing back to me
a fuller life
of a faith that never fails.
    in the twilight
just beginning
there is an instant,
never ending,
when we go off
and spinning
out across the milky way.
in the darkness
always turning
towards the light
of another morning
comes a moment
without warning
when we're finally

on our way.

    in the ages

that are fast approaching

there are those

who awake unknowing,

on a journey

from which they

can never stray.

while here

in this dim light of evening

i lie half asleep,

rocking

in the cradle of another day.

    yes,

there are no words

to the tune

that my grandfather's

mother's humming,

while to the beat

beneath my legs,

someone else's

feet are running

towards a field

of far off stars
to where
Orion's child is coming.
yes, winter's
eastern sky at night
sends home to earth
man's delight.
on heavenly wings
of ancestral light,
Orion's child is coming.
  elsewhere
is Orion's child,
in whose heart
the hunters' pulse
is pounding,
beating out a rhythm
of ten thousand years
in every newborn's cry
resounding
with a fullness
which draws us near
to the center
of a universe

that's expanding,

until in the silence

left behind

we arrive

at a better understanding

of who and where

and what we are,

and why the creator

is not demanding

that we take our position

among those stars

and reach out

for the hand

that's extending.

    yes, elsewhere

is this god of mine,

at the speed of light

reclining,

at rest

on a sea of sighs,

in each breath

deciding

whether or not

to be here

among us now,

where that moment

of departure

is always

almost arriving.

    ice

water

ice

is an endless flow.

    ice

water

ice

is forever more.

    yes we are

ice water ice

until we are

just once more,

    ice.

heaven's company

     in silence
echoing silence
without any
storied words to tell
by shadow over shadow
in alliance
the she of darkness
has cast her spell
with hands that reach
out across the ages
to close a net
webbed both strong and fine
she draws us together
like so many fishes
fresh from the oceans of time.
     with the moon and stars
as her bright lit companions
she searches her catch
for the ones that know of light
then taking their eyes
as bait for others

sets off again

into the depths of night.

    blinded now

i lie upon the shore

where i can feel

the rise of the tide

no more

sinking heavily

into the sand

i've come at last

to understand

what it takes

to be a free born man

and why

the she of darkness

has no use at all

for those

who will not answer

ancient light's gripping call

or in other words

as she's often said

without heaven's company

you're better off dead.

the she of darkness
works against the veil
to reproduce salvation
in every detail
at the time of crossing
she is honor bound
to resurrect the pathways
between sight and sound
on her friendship
every future dawning
will depend
so near the waters' edge
i wait for her again
to return
as she once said she might
bringing with her
for me
the gift of second sight.
      (prepare)
prepare to strike
the earth by shouting
said the god child
as he raised his staff

be quick

to turn your face away

if my eyes

begin to laugh.

everything

comes from somewhere

just where this is

do not dare to ask

for it takes

more than every fiber

in your body

to be equal

to the task

of reviving revelation

from the insights

of the past

so as to arrive

whole in time

upon the plains

of departation

from within

this moment's

monumental grasp.

to be there

where the anthems

of entitlement

spring full-blown

from memory's

abyssal lapse

as the articulated embrace

of innate wisdom

makes up

in ways unknown

for all that reason lacks.

    come!

take a walk with me

we shall seek

this heaven's company

come

let us talk

of being free

that our ears

might become eyes

to see

the synchronicity of infinity

at least momentarily.

separate entity

there were beetles sleeping
beneath the bark of that log
as i laid it gently on the fire
tell me
did they dream away the last of life
or awake suddenly
there on their funeral pyre
(high overhead
in another world
eyes of the hunting hawk
circling
settle on a rabbit)
when hunger comes
we search each day
with vision born out of habit.

oh, deep restless
spirit wind
surge in ambush
from within
break through that mist

which shrouds us in sin
shake loose this grip
on my mortal skin
allow the earth
to enmesh us as a friend
rattle and drum up
a moment of peace again
by granting to these wings
the power on which they depend
oh! Deep Restless Spirit Wind!

that wind is like a river
headed to the sea
darkness always guides the blind
in times of facing eternity
are we really worth the effort
it takes to be free
if all around us
lives must turn to dust
while feeding a voracious reality.
in the heart of a hunter
there lives another
a lover of immense enormity

whose magnitude is open to view

through the dying eyes

of a separate entity

standing on the edge

of a one-way bridge

at torrent of dreams

beneath my feet

with the sky as my guide

the farthest reaches are inside

unpeopled by the faces that i meet.

   pack away no altar cloth

but bring the moon and stars

and together with the instincts of innocence

we shall tour the galaxies

 in search of what once was ours

a knot of hair

a path of stone

a graveyard dream

we called our own

a distant time

from which this place has grown

breaking us open

right on the edge of believing.

a book of shadows

fell open upon the table

with a fire burning

brightly in the stove

each moment spoke

of forgotten measures

another world's lost treasure trove.

who will drink deep

the draught of honeyed water?

who can taste

tomorrow's lightness on the tongue?

where goes the heartbeat

of every instant

when we listen

to the rhythm of songs unsung

can you evoke?

the circles of breath returning

to a voice

that's birthing in the dark

will you rejoice?

in the vistas of innate learning

please now

tip your candle to the spark

for we are all tallow, wax, and fiber

shaped by a swirl of celestial wind

forever to be muted, boundless beauty

filling with emptiness from within.

banquet of winter

the wind is a giant
who sometimes sleeps
with one eye open
for those he might meet
at the banquet of winter
where the cold comes to feast
on the flesh of the dreamers
who fall into sleep
too deep.

the fire is a wizard
with many secrets to keep
with hunger in his heart
he takes all he can eat
and turns it to ashes
to smoke and to heat
to cook from my bones
his portion of meat
to cast a spell
that when finally complete
wraps me in armor
that none can defeat.

this earth is a savior

unable to preach

to those who have ears

or the power of speech

emptied of melody

the rhythms take shape

a message of harmony

for us to translate

   the wind is a giant

make no mistake

asleep there is music

that is not

for those who are awake.

    on the eastern edge

of an inward sea

awash in a tidal wave

of memory

ancestral currents arise in me

eclipsing the echo of eternity.

    on a ridge all alone

through that darkness

headed home

in my throat wolves still live

even though i have no howl to give.

shrugging my shoulders

the oak trees bend

a thousand pictures painted

in the language of the wind

embryonic voices torn

from the tongues of men

join together in unison

to strike a chord within.

  songs of extinction fill the air

alive with an inheritance we each can share

our eventual destination is empty at the end

for our bodies carry a tune

that no mind can comprehend,

  but when our final whisperings draw silence

and that music is about to begin

tell me

who will be there to listen

as that last note awakens

all the natural born dreamers

from sleep walking

once again?

on the way to stardust
where do the rivers flow
on the way who can tell me
where do they go
on the way to stardust
how often does this world divide
before the earth and sun
finally collide
on the way to stardust
where are those
who bring this coming age
of stardust to a close?

margaret rose

    the doorway to mystery
opens with a combination lock
unseen
the ceiling of the sky only
over shadows
the planking of my heart
there is no air
beyond our breathing
in this single chambered spot
where waiting as the tumblers fall
we listen for love to start
    trapped among the briars
on a sunny berry slope
late afternoon showers splatter
the ancient odor of a primal hope
in the midst of rocks and hunger
i move with the utmost care
under the spell of the living
i turn and taste the air
when tomorrow comes a calling
will love find me there

in that pulsating, magnetic sensation

which both pulls and pushes apart

for that's always been the way

of recirculating memories

in a new born multi-chambered

heart.

portage of the soul

I. open handed hold

life
with eyes wide open
and memory intact
open handed hold
on recalling birth
at the mystery of the gates
cold day dawning
treeless plain
ellipse of stone
smoothest incline
breathless passage
wind stilled waves
eternity awaits
who can say more?
sleeper in the cave
earth and seed together
warmest embrace
source of all beginnings
portage of the soul!

fire lit eyes

trembling touch

good journey again.

II. ancient island

oh ancient island

source of mystery

stand fast

in the spirit seas

moonset at morning

rainbows come midday

deep wind stirs

newborn voices into song

fire eating wood

flowing water everywhere

shadows kiss the ground

to open evening into darkness

treetops bright with sleep

sweep heaven earthward

silent the deer women bow

unfleshed the great stag weeps

how full is the heart

knowing

the sky is blue?

III. space within

    the old tree seems empty

now that the deer is gone

nine long days and nights

we hung there

nose

three feet from the ground

even the neighborhood squirrels and jays

grew accustomed to the view

but now when the wind enters

this clearing at dawn

it hesitates for a moment

before passing on through

    yes, the old tree seems empty

now that death has gone

see how the branches rattle and tremble

as if to point a finger towards the sun

do they know (that for them) a darkness

beyond the loss of leaves is yet to come

do they know of a winter so deep

that from the icy depths of its frozen heart

no spring has ever sprung?

    yes, the old tree seems so empty

even the sky is torn

ripped open along the scars

left over from that day

the earth was born

how long?

must this sacred space within

now wear a crown of thorns

a ring of sorrows to defend

our greatest natural talent

from those heavenly virtues

we leave unformed

    yes the old tree is empty

still, life must go on

and with it

those who believe in mystery

are given breath enough

to greet another dawn

for while the traveler

finds rest in splendor

the native takes release
in a moment from beyond
and when the two
finally grow together
no power in eternity
can last as long
    the old tree is empty
nothing now to do
but watch and wait
as the advent of fate
turns inside out
every point of view
given the merits
of the human race
a need for a savior
is no disgrace
still it's about time
so let's just ask
to inherit something new
    yes the old is empty
marvelous and full
across a threshold of paradox
is where spirit is inclined to go

out beyond the event horizon

leads the portage of the soul

on into the watersheds of the mother ocean

where willful unknowing

(as a reasonable feeling of emptiness)

is both in and out of control

    the old is empty

and so is the new

together giving birth

to an ancient timeless future moment

where the light touch of immortality

is in eternal darkness renewed

for the secret of becoming one

is the same as being two

as the loyalty of life to itself

is in death forever true

    look to the trees

        look and see

    the old is new.

(for the culmination

of evolution is involution.)

taken to raise

i returned
from the hills of night
to light a fire
in the rain
while all around
unseen phantoms watched
with delight
as the splinters glowed
then broke unbounded
into flame
to call the wind
now at my back
from more than miles away
i edged towards
the sizzling ash
and completely went astray
fire eyes
of a spirits face
gazing outward know
every hidden hollowed place
where rising voices grow

crackling embers

demand a sacrifice

crying out

for a little something

from us all

yet who's to say

what's really at stake

when the dream milkers

come to call

    since that time

i've left my home

and the wind

has taken me to raise

cold and hunger

know me as their own

and share with me

the benefit of their days

    now when the dream milkers

come at night

to feed on those emotions of old

they find me quiet

by the firelight

doing exactly

as i am told
    simply
by the tilt of my head
while i pat
this earth at my side
i give to them
their only dread
daggers from my eyes
cut and bleeding
they stumble away
surprising each other
with their new-found cries
which are the first
and only truthful part
of what's been a lifetime
full of lies
    for far too long
they have roamed at will
be satisfying their thirst
with our tears
in stirring up hatred all around
they grow strong
for as long as we run

from our fears

but now i'm the one

who follows them

to bring an end

to their count of years

an end that waits

down this trail of twisted words

that are verbal swords

made up of broken mirrors.

twice born

i am a bard of lineage
twice born from the same mother
twin seats of equal power
clan of the Dragon
clan of the Jaguar
forged in the face of focused harmony
fused through the friction formed
when my future being came into me
i am a bard of lineage
mistake me for no other
think me not my sister's brother
or my children's father
i am a bard of lineage
my home is the word unspoken
my journey
the promise unbroken
to bring tomorrow into being
to guide the blind into seeing
to call forth in the disbelieving
a most inescapable feeling
which opens the heart to receiving

the essence of those who are asleep and dreaming

of awakening around a circle kneeling

while crying for the vision we are needing

to give new blood to the ones

who have half-begun their leavings

from this world of lifetimes

of mistaken achieving

nothing, absolutely nothing.

    i am a bard of lineage

    twice born of the same mother

    mistake me for no other

    i am my spirit's double.

this

i've never met a bitter wind
or one that could make me cry
but someday before this breath is through
that boast will turn into a lie
for there are so many clouds
broken on every horizon
from a whirlwind way up in the sky
that i can see right now, without a doubt
i must change to stay alive
    ever since i was a little child
i've looked each wind right in the eye
for i was born to be a weathered man
shaped by every storm front which passes by
be it a cold white winter's dawn
or a summer's darkest.midnight rain
never before this have i felt myself a part
of any crazy god's pointless game
    like a wolf who watches in the night
at his distant relatives being fed
by man's artificial fire light
i've grown accustomed

to judging wrong from right

by this feeling which holds me at bay

    even though the bed is warm

and the food is good

i know these will not bring me whole

into being who i should

and therefore i must turn

to go the other way

    long ago most of mankind gave away

what is precious from inside us

and now the rest tries to steal from me

the strength of a thunder storm decided

when all i am is bent on reaching the earth

this very day

    so that in the coming period

of restructuring vital energies

during the movement devoted

to consuming precious memories

as images from others

begin to close in on me

i can still plant my feet

and spinning face them fearlessly

to drive each and every thought

back into that world

from which it came

and then if the spirit of eternity

should seek again to speak with me

i will be able to greet it immediately

a knife between my teeth

blood already dripping from the blade

disembodied words can cut or kill

if you don't believe me

just try me and i'll show you that they will

leaving someone stumbling

a foot already in the grave

    ego driven rhetoric

is often pointless and childish

but the tongue of a true man

can be as sharpened and as dangerous

as the devils his kindest words

lay in wait to slay

so tell me - do you hear me?

can you catch

can you stop

the edge of what it is

i've labored so to say?

passage back

a chair! a chair!
i need a chair
to sit here
by the table there
oh yes, you see
i found a table
before i was me
and that's not all i found
i found a candle
with night all around
and when i fixed myself
upon the sight
i found that i was the light
or was it that the light was me?
either way is how it has to be
because there is no reason
because there is no me
there is no me, don't you see?
sitting here upon this chair
next to that table which is not there
yet in the coming darkness i can see

fast approaching what once was me

for when i stand within the night

must i not also know of light

and if i am not myself

am i then someone else?

if an answer is what you seek

question first those you meet

guarding the portals of your sleep

for it is only in our dreams

that the water's clear

life is big

and the sky is near

it's only in your dreams

that you'll ever hear

what these words

really have to say

for as the master gives

the giver takes

as the sleeper dreams

the dreamer awakes

to the certainty

that life will never forsake

the memory that awaits

the unborn children

of the human race

    if i say it once more in rhyme

after seeing life ignite

one hundred times

will i reveal with brightness

in a thousand ways

a feeling which burns

a candle of ten million days

for each succeeding generation

receives a repeating invitation

to far exceed their own expectations

by arriving at the realization

that before perception there is sensation

yes, before perception there is sensation

and so by way of simple demonstration

one day life leaves us without an explanation

    no form or substance real or solid

no oath to give or allegiance to follow

no way to end once you've started

greeting life open hearted

pressed between the earth and sun

with jolting grace the jester runs

seeking asylum and finding none

any where along the way

while overhead, out of sight

beyond the reach of day and night

behind our sun countless stars blaze.

    more to this than can be known

yet nothing less than what is shown

at the center of a stellar furnace we all began

now returning on the event horizon

all that any of us can say is, simply,

i am.

silhouetted against the sun

a blazing fire my life's become

which one among these flames i see

 is that eternal spark that's really me

encamped beneath a starless sky

bands of angles come strolling by

each one with their begging bowl

hungry for my desperate soul

each one seeks the same reply

yet who on earth can decide

what price passage back into paradise?

quadrants

   i do not grow shallow

as i fall silent

while riding from the rim

to the hub

of the wheel of fate

for i am the spokesman

who has dissected the circle

by cutting a cross

into the middle

in order to reinstate

outward momentum

draped

over an inner movement

which stirs up

the still point

while working to recirculate

all that's before me

into something

forever behind me

as that moment

comes quickly

where the hour seems late

no i do not grow shallow

as i fall silent

though it might be easy

to make a mistake

and think me

blind, broken and feeble

when in truth

i'm simply stopping

to contemplate

the ways of returning

to an unspoken center

where gravity

will balance out

my spinning weight

by overturning

this feeling of falling

while uncovering

a rolling productive gait

which travels this earth

in search of remembering

the beginnings of building

that wheel of fate

where i first fell shallow

as i grew silent

while moving from the hub

to the rim

of this ancient spiral

we all create

  if i seem shallow

because i am silent

know

that i've learned

how to watch and wait

as that wheel of fortune

dips down deep inside me

and gathers up again

it once and future

bending shape

that everyday

cuts a track straight

into the heartland of tomorrow

by agreement with the contours

of time and space

until just one single thought

emptied of ambition and desire

counters with a revolution

centered

on a pivot of momentary grace

than all shall be silent

and none will be shallow

as the echo

of these words

tumble into place

and the hum

of that still spinning axle

vanishes

into mid-air

with barely a trace

    for yes i am the spokesman

who knows

the quadrants

and can draw out the appearance

needed to imitate

natures prowess

for living the riddles

which speak directly

to the unformed forces

we must one day

turn and face

    that is to say

the wisdom of the ancients

is based on quadrants

then sealed in ceremonies

composed from nothingness

at a rapid rate

so that no one personality

can adversely reflect reality

when all of everything

is equally made.

    so, no

i do not grow shallow

even though

i will now fall silent

riding again the rim

of this wheel of fate.

About the Author

Joseph Samuel Plum is a direct descendant of Welsh bards and Native American spirit. He lives in South Central Iowa within a group of trees where he composes and presents bardic poetry of original nature. He has been doing this for fifty years. This is his ninth book.

Books by Joseph S. Plum:

RELICS

CONCENTRIC DEVOTION

LANDMASS AND OTHER POEMS

STAR SIGHT GATHERING

WHERE RISING VOICES GROW

HUMAN LANDSCAPE

NOBLE REMNANTS

BOOK OF SHADOWS

OLD PATH

www.JoePlum.com

www.ingramcontent.com/pod-product-compliance
Lightning Source LLC
Chambersburg PA
CBHW051709090426
42736CB00013B/2608